MW00510200

This Notebook Belongs To